MOPES
KENNETH REVEIZ

FENCE BOOKS

Book Design: Ramon Tejada / El Estudio de Ramon, in collaboration
with Kenneth Reveiz, using the typefaces GT Alpina, GT Alpina
Typewriter, and GT Ultra by Grilli Type, and Courier by Howard
Kettler. This book was printed at Puritan Capital in NH and
distributed by Small Press Distribution and Consortium.

Image credit: Photo that appears on page 76 is a screenshot of an
image credited to Survival International/Reuters from 2008.

Published in the United States by
Fence Books
110 Union Street
Second Floor
Hudson, NY 12534
fenceportal.org

Library of Congress Cataloguing in Publication Data
Reveiz, Kenneth [1990-]
MOPES / Kenneth Reveiz

Library of Congress Control Number: 2022941556
ISBN 13: 978-1-944380-24-3

First Edition
10 9 8 7 6 5 4 3 2

for camila maría concepción

The artist ought to be distinguished by selfless devotion to duty;

but we forgot about that a long time ago.

ACT ONE

INTERMISSION

ACT TWO

SECOND INTERMISSION

ACT THREE

ACT

O N E

White people playing music
White people booking shows
White people writing news stories
White people talking to white people about white people

White people at the museum
White people taking pictures with white people
White people teaching young adults
White people teaching people of color about white people

White people in graduate programs
White people being professional with other white people
White people using iPhones
White people watching movies made by white people with white people in them

White people taking up too much space in a room full of other people
White people building luxury apartments in a neighborhood where white people don't live
White people selling objects to people of color
White people jarring honey

White people farming
White people publishing stuff by white people bought by white people
White people playing sousaphone
White people falling in love with white people

White people treating people of color like shit
White people calling people of color racist
White people touching the bodies of other white people and people of color without their consent
White people expecting people of color to do what they want them to do

White people dressing business casual
White people thinking that the justice system is actually just
White people dancing like people of color
White people frantically sending emails

White people hiring white people
White people going on vacation
White people scheduling the school reform meeting during school when people in school can't be
there
White people posting music and videos and news articles by white people on social media

White people starting wars with countries that are primarily made up of people of color
White people believing in objectivity
White people making decisions big and small
White people shushing people of color

White people making art   and putting it everywhere   unapologetically

*I'm still waiting for this person from True Colors to get back to me and confirm, she hasn't gotten
back to me in four days. But if she comes to talk about the black, lesbian person and her relation
to the Matthew Shepard case ten years later, we can get the, you know, um, ethno-social side. You
know what, Kenneth, I know that there are a ton of issues that need to be discussed. There are so
many people who could talk on the high school panel about queer theory. And I know there's all this
trans stuff. I get that. I get that there are a lot of things that we could cover. The thing is, we only
have 50 minutes for this panel. We need to focus on the most important things.*

White people drinking beer
White people doing drugs
White people owning businesses
White people drinking coffee

White people on the one hand calling their co-worker who is a person of color who was not born in
the U.S. "a bitch" and on the other hand to another, younger person of color who was born in the U.S.
outwardly performing friendship
White people organizing events, publications, and institutions addressing the lives of people who
are not them but not resourcing those people—people who would know better than white people
about their own lives—to lead and to act
White people pretending to be nice
White people managing employees and/or volunteers who are people of color

White people informing people of color of the decisions that they made without people of color—
decisions that will vastly affect the housing, neighborhoods, jobs, and daily lives of people of color
—and not expecting uproar and animosity but instead to be complimented for their brilliance and
what's more mastery and virtuosity in matters of urban design
White people using terminology when referring to the social and political life of people of color
internationally, such as "they need more economic development" or "they're underdeveloped" or
"that's exactly why they're still a Third World country," not only presuming that theirs is the best
or only social and economic model but furthermore that that social and economic model is even
desirable to these people who have been psychologically terrorized and economically fucked over

precisely by that social and economic model and its culture that perpetuates and ignores histories of colonialism, imperialism, mineral exploitation, workforce exploitation, and military intervention, all which led to the field that is being implicated as inherently inferior in the first place. A useful word for this is "crypto-racist."

White people who only have friends who are white people
White people who only date people who are white people
White people confused by the idea of white privilege and, in an arrogant display of publicly denying white privilege, articulating precisely the problematic embeddedness of the reality of white privilege
White people reviewing art by people of color that challenges the dominant structures of power and calling it bad art

White people renovating houses
White people threatening to evict people of color
White people making movies with white people killing people of color in them
White people working at not-for-profits

White people using people of color as accessories in order to enact desired narratives in their social lives
White people not tipping
White people projecting monster dynamics onto people of color
White people inculcating disposability, replaceability, self-doubt, and worthlessness into the psyche of people of color

White people who have access to adequate housing, healthcare, employment, transportation, finances, leisure, upward mobility, representation in narratives, institutions, and ideologies and finally a sense of what is possible for them individually and in groups and collectively a ellos ni siquiera les ocurre that people of color should share the same access to housing, healthcare, employment, transportation, finances, leisure, upward mobility, representation in narratives, institutions, and ideologies and a sense of what is possible for them individually and in groups and collectively

White people buying stocks
White people reading bedtime stories about white people
White people being Eurocentric
White people thinking that everything they produce is universal

White people having sex
White people having babies
White people eating Chinese food, Mexican food, Ethiopian food
White people getting in touch with their heritages

White people mentoring countless other white people but not even a single person of color
White people taking classes like history and literature and visual art and learning about history and literature and visual art made by white people and what white people thought about it
White people going to museums whose curators are white people and whose art was created by white people
White people saying things on every subject including people of color with authority

White people thinking they could never be rejected romantically or sexually by people of color
White people feeling entitled to claim the labor of people of color
White people feeling entitled to the land that people of color live on
White people feeling entitled to the bodies that are the bodies of people of color

White people victimizing themselves
White people being scared
White people travelling to countries that are majority people of color
White people not being deported

White people not paying taxes
White people not being arrested
White people winning awards
White people being applauded for treating docile people of color with dignity

White people resenting the power people of color have
White people punishing people of color who say no to them
White people trying to destroy people of color with power, or talent, or vision
White people creating a narrative of incompetence and laziness and corruption around perfectly competent, hard-working, and honest people of color

White people with weird-ass energy
White people lying and getting away with it
White people thinking they always deserve to win
White people acting like they don't know any better when they do

White people being mean
White people getting law degrees
White people thinking they know better than people of color
White people learning Spanish and acting like it makes them Latino

White people asking you for your pronouns and then misgendering you anyway
White people grabbing objects with ferocious intensity
White people exercising
White people confusing solidarity with friendship

White people paying people of color to clean up after them and their businesses
White people making money
White people committing wage theft
White people who are police officers harassing and killing

White people being produced
White people being published
White people gaslighting people of color or trying to
White people not wanting people of color to lead much less even help solve a problem

White people being uncomfortable, recognizing their privileges, and using their power to give people of color and poor people and queer and trans people and women and femmes and indigenous folks a tremendous amount of agency over our collective lives and institutions and environment

White people commodifying the magic people of color have
White people not helping people of color translate or understand English in medical settings
White people laughing at media representations or TV shows or movies with people of color in them that people of color do not laugh at because the laughter is one of crypto-superiority
White people not asking what people of color whom they claim to want to support and empower need and want and helping them attain those things but rather pursuing their own assigned solutions, problems, and processes, or in fact not doing anything at all

White people feeling entitled to the resources that people of color have

"But aren't you just being divisive? Aren't you just being reverse racist? Divisiveness never solves anything. You need to be more professional and reasonable."

This is precisely the language of unmarkedness, where the feeling of a sharing of power occurs, and should be embraced. You must embrace our ignorance, and cultural poverty, and brashness, in order that you can confront your own ignorance, and cultural poverty, and brashness.

And whoever said that poetry and art don't have to be anything but beautiful and useless, they are a poem, they are a work of art.

GEGENÜBER

(Schwules Museum)

In conclusion waiting
favoring the places where i feel the least distance from you:
    your bed,
                your arms,
        the beds that you sleep in,
            the mouth that you
          use to kiss me and the
        other things you have kissed

the discourse is one   always   of desire
    distance   but the course
            is to be
                near to you
even the cliché of the heart
    the goal   to be inside it
      the built   prism   triangle
    orange   maples   circle
      spaces with you   and me   in them
    the space of thought   water
        memory even or especially

to lose this you   that i feel i have
    and want not to have but have
would be   fuck
the beginning   of a kiss
    or your cum   on my face
the cum that you do not have
    placed onto me
or the time   that i want
that i spent
    or else passed
      with you
that i loved   or now
      love
    or now feel   that i loved
walking with you   eating at

the same time   smiling
your grunt   on my chest
        the grunting that you made

there is time   that i passed with
                              you
    it occurred   and it is nice
        to know that you are a thing in my life
that i like to have in my life
and want to have more in my life
        as things occur   or do not
but mostly do   all the time
        they would be   prism   song
air   good taste world   even sky
even stars

water goes into my mouth
through my lips
        the mouth that i have
the things that you have and are
        thing that i love
things that i feel
        about you
                that are
                        good
that make me feel good

i know that i will fail under the wrong paradigms
                                        you know
                                many things
        that you have lived through
                and passed   the mouth that i have
        the cock that i have
        the touches you have applied to it
                have made it feel good
        the rubbing   the mouth that you have
                the skin on your body the kiss
        i apply   to your face   to your cock
                to the face that you have
            that you had at that time

seeing people walking that i have seen walking at other times

                                                    that i have walked with
is a nice thing   a thing that makes me feel good
smile happens   i did not exactly feel   happening
that smile   that i felt   happened
        that happened on the face that does not belong to me but that i have

the color of the sky is many colors a very small
amount of water on the neck
            on the arm on the finger
on the arm on the finger
    that is part of my
on the arm body

i am not sure of anything but
    i know a lot of things
the rain isn't   exactly   falling
        it is and has   been
onto me   from the distance
    from some distance   lengths
that i've measured   often
        with the weakest and queerest empiricisms
or not   they have the useless map too
feelings occur   and they are fucking amazing
    not in the middle of in any thing en
        of but and vagueness or something
not the idea or the meaning even or
        even the feeling   but a the
                most fucking amazing fully distanceless thing

DISSPOEM

EXT. NEW YORK CITY STREET - DAY

DMX's "X Gon Give it To Ya" plays. BRETT (30s, white) and
VERONICA (30s, white) begin their killing competition.

RESTAURANT

Veronica grabs a grenade, stuffs it up a KID's ass, and
punts the kid into a crowded restaurant, which EXPLODES.

A death counter appears on the bottom right of the screen.
V: 23 B: 0. We cut to a

GAS STATION

where Brett, in SLOW MOTION, leaps at a MAN. Brett draws
his FISH from his back holster where it's been sheathed
like a samurai sword. Spinning in the air, with a wet slap
Brett knocks the man into a SCHOOL BUS, which swerves into
a gas station and EXPLODES. **V: 23 B: 18.** In front of a

BIG BOX STORE

Veronica slices a woman in half. The woman SPLITS APART,
revealing an advertisement that reads **"50% OFF."** Veronica
then throws her sword through a GUY's neck, impaling him.
He falls backwards and impales the three people behind
him. They all fall onto a fire hydrant, which blasts open,
first blasting their bodies hundreds of feet in the air,
then blasting a jet of water into a stroller, smashing
it into a wall. The sword falls from the sky, is caught
by Veronica's waiting hand. The bodies then land around
Veronica in a perfect, circular synchronized-swimming-
esque formation. **V: 28 B: 18.**

PARKING LOT

Brett, fish back on his back, pulls out his SPOON. He
swipes at a GUY's head, which opens up, revealing his
brains and eyeballs. Brett catapults each eyeball at a car
—and each car EXPLODES. He sticks the spoon into a LITTLE
GIRL's mouth and hurls her into a wall. He then throws the
spoon into the side of a gasoline truck, which EXPLODES.
The spoon shoots back through the air - and is caught by
Brett's waiting HAND. **V: 28 B: 25.**

PLAYGROUND

Veronica pulls out her GUN, aims at a playground, and
shoots each kid in the forehead. She smirks, having easily
secured her lead again. **V: 36 B: 25.**

GAS STATION PUMP

Sweating, Brett pulls out his fish, runs over to a gasoline
pump which is shooting gasoline out in a jet, and places the
fish's mouth over the hole. He fills his fish with gasoline.
Brett clamps the fish's mouth shut with his hand, dashes
over to some stunned TOURISTS, sparks a lighter, and fires a
BLAST of flaming gasoline at the tourists, who run around ON
FIRE until they collapse. One of them runs into a speeding
taxi and both BLOW UP, the taxi twisting high IN THE AIR.
We see a KID, standing in the middle of all this massacre,
terrified. A SHADOW appears below him, then grows larger
and larger. He LOOKS UP, whimpers, and the tourist-fish-
gasoline-explosion taxi CRASHES down onto him. **V: 36 B: 37.**
Brett cheers, realizing he has taken the lead. Determined,
Veronica spots a

SCHOOL FIELD TRIP GROUP

Veronica runs through the school field trip group, swinging
her sword wildly. When she emerges from the crowd, she
looks back and sees the dead. On her sword are a few of the
children — it's a kindergartener shish kabeb. She slides the
kids off her sword. **V: 68 B: 37.**

Brett speeds off in a MOTORCYCLE. In the distance is a

CHUCKY CHEESE

Brett, full speed ahead on the bike, aims at the Chucky
Cheese, and he does a backflip off the bike. We see a wide
shot of the Chucky Cheese, Brett nailing his landing and
facing the camera. The inside of the Chucky Cheese fills with
flames and the glass EXPLODES outward. Brett turns around;
A FLAMING PIECE OF PEPPERONI PIZZA is pasted to his ass. He
peels it off and takes a bite. **V: 68 B: 77.**

Veronica meanwhile is PARAGLIDING over the city. She swoops
downwards at incredible speed, SWORD pointed at a

DUNKIN DONUTS

A COP is walking out, eating a donut. Veronica flies towards
him with the sword but the cop dodges it, and her sword gets
stuck in a wall, cracking the building's foundation. The cop
punches at Veronica. Veronica dodges. She lurches forward
vampire-like and takes a bite out of his neck. He screams in
agony. The building has begun to rumble. Veronica dropkicks
the cop into the Dunkin, which CRUMBLES to the ground
around him. Veronica LEAPS AWAY from the growing cloud of
dust and rubble, diving through a window and into a SWIMMING

POOL. She emerges from the water, and sensuously flips her hair. **V: 100 B: 77.**

HOSPITAL EMERGENCY ENTRANCE IN RUSSIA

Brett faces a RANDOM GUY who is armed with a machine gun. Brett pulls out his FISH and blocks an entire magazine of bullets with it, which utterly destroys his fish.

The guy, out of machine gun ammo, pulls out a pistol and Brett pulls out his spoon. The guy fires seven shots, each one deflected by a swiping of Brett's spoon. Each of the bullets fly into AMBULANCES, which EXPLODE.

Brett angrily holds his spoon, sharing a mutual STARE OF HATE with the guy.

Brett tosses the spoon away and RUNS at the guy. In SLOW MOTION, he leaps and flips over the guy's head. Brett pulls off the UNDERWEAR that he's been wearing over his pants the whole time and, still in mid-air, pulls the underwear over the guy's head, leaving the guy fumbling for sight. The underwear BEEPS … and EXPLODES. **V: 100 B: 100.**

Veronica looks at the score, looks at an OLD WOMAN standing dumbfounded in the middle of all the destruction, and looks back at the score. She runs at the woman really fast -and PUNTS her over a skyscraper. The woman GLIMMERS LIKE A STAR in the night sky. **V: 101 B: 100.** Veronica smiles.

blue sun

responsibility

we have to share our most distorted and honest poems with
everyone who cares to listen because the dinosaur lives
and we are born in the footprints of white supremacy culture
the smiling heterosexual couple crosses the street towards
        me and dildos fall from the branches of the trees
        that someone chose should be seen there in a line
                                        ecomilitarily
the poem must be responsible and raw and honest and
precise, here we are, this is the alienatedly world as
it can be seen and, exhaustingly until all people do it
all the time, the not made and undistributed poster or
directionless but well-intended campaign or bitchiness or
bullshit or loud noise that betrays the power you feel you

have lost, but it is exhaustingly organization and cultural
warfare and non-normativity that will unalienatedly the mute
world

The boy shows off his blood for everyone's approval while i
chase him with a roll of paper towels and a cup of water
The people judge his action, this sight and decision, in
small groups
or as individuals
or as individuals in small groups
Some think he's wack
some think he's cool
others think other things
rare is the person who says what she thinks about the blood
which dries under the leather jacket that he now wears
What do you think?

educated people of the world, who have been trained to check
e-mail daily, and respond to them, who know the difference
between their they're and there, who buy snacks, who may see
psychotherapists, who believe in progress, who believe in first
world countries, who complain about stupid shit, it is not
okay to project an image that you have onto someone else and
address them as that image which is not what they said they
are who they are — I am not someone to speak Spanish to unless
it's obvious we should be doing that, I am no longer someone
to pity as suicidal or troubled because i'm the gayest, I do
not see marriage as equality what the fuck is marriage anyway
but bourgeois counter-revolutionary, I do not think the kids
want your afterschool program because it is not an afterschool
program that they had anything to do with wanting or making
and is in fact kind of racist, they do not want your economic
development because they are not undeveloped.   Astoria,
where I grew up writing screenplays and playing soccer with my
brother or poor and Latino writing screenplays and playing
soccer with my brother, and the high rises are now empty as
the young white people jog in the their beautiful Fordham
sweaters at night. Fordham University twenty times and it
becomes Astoria. The image becomes the space. The space becomes
the image. Fair Haven is amazing.   Latina older woman of
ambiguous race kisses ambiguously gendered Latina person
checking in about lover of ambiguous race and/or gender. Latina
older woman of ambiguous race kisses ambiguously gendered
Latina person checking in about lover of ambiguous race and/
or gender.   Latina older woman of ambiguous race kisses
ambiguously gendered Latina person checking in about lover of

ambiguous race and/or gender. Latina older woman of ambiguous race kisses ambiguously gendered Latina person checking in about lover of ambiguous race and/or gender. Latina older woman of ambiguous race kisses ambiguously gendered Latina person checking in about lover of ambiguous race and/or gender. Latina older woman of ambiguous race kisses ambiguously gendered Latina person checking in about lover of ambiguous race and/or gender. Latina older woman of ambiguous race kisses ambiguously gendered Latina person checking in about lover of ambiguous race and/or gender. Latina older woman of ambiguous race kisses ambiguously gendered Latina person checking in about lover of ambiguous race and/or gender. Latina older woman of ambiguous race kisses ambiguously gendered Latina person checking in about lover of ambiguous race and/or gender. Latina older woman of ambiguous race kisses ambiguously gendered Latina person checking in about lover of ambiguous race and/or gender. Latina older woman of ambiguous race kisses ambiguously gendered Latina person checking in about lover of ambiguous race and/or gender. Latina older woman of ambiguous race kisses ambiguously gendered Latina person checking in about lover of ambiguous race and/or gender. Latina older woman of ambiguous race kisses ambiguously gendered Latina person checking in about lover of ambiguous race and/or gender. Latina older woman of ambiguous race kisses ambiguously gendered Latina person checking in about lover of ambiguous race and/or gender. Latina older woman of ambiguous race kisses ambiguously gendered Latina person checking in about lover of ambiguous race and/or gender. Latina older woman of ambiguous race kisses ambiguously gendered Latina person checking in about lover of ambiguous race and/or gender. Latina older woman of ambiguous race kisses ambiguously gendered Latina person checking in about lover of ambiguous race and/or gender. Latina older woman of ambiguous race kisses ambiguously gendered Latina person checking in about lover of ambiguous race and/or gender. Latina older woman of ambiguous race kisses ambiguously gendered Latina person checking in about lover of ambiguous race and/or gender. Latina older woman of ambiguous race kisses ambiguously gendered Latina person checking in about lover of ambiguous race and/or gender. Latina older woman of ambiguous race kisses ambiguously gendered Latina person checking in about lover of ambiguous race and/or gender. Latina older woman of ambiguous race kisses ambiguously gendered Latina person checking in about lover of ambiguous race and/or gender.

I could have said a million things. I won't say them now. They are not the best things I can be saying to you right now.

Because I can, I make the choice to use language — to say, for instance, that people suffer for your belief that anything could ever be apolitical. They suffer for this belief that you have or encourage, that anything could ever be apolitical. Then they suffer, responsibility, blue sun, for our actions and inactions.

Interm

ission

FLESH

i do not want what i have to say,
the light on your face, to be
ignored, i even could love you

strengthlessness ubiquitous, iterating quiet
step, tender debris,
            the fang thud, restlessly sight, flesh entirely wound
            damp and unachievedly
of the murmur that i've been, so that I neatly am

        some thing
                sobjects
        somewhere
                with brilliant logic

                        cloud all unsolid and intangible-like, stupid
                    lonely,
and it's funny that, with half with my body hacked off from my mind and the land, there
cave and light thru, not us but how surrendered, because i'm mastered not skying not
water:
                    slow blue
            hands' fever   firm ridge
        begging for resolution or something i don't know, imperceptibility,
                even feeling
                    I'd like to feel it I really would

i'll say it again—   expanses exists, and is beyond a thing
when chopped the down try bird and branch in my mouth or anything,
e-mails that exists and is a things, it was, all where the vast blue sky and cluds or
whatever i'm in I, looking at the world, with and you are too, maybe, about, and
are there's always ruins in the distance that are here too, as well, tierra tambiendo
siendo flesh

& it is. but also what
it isn't, and what it nearly
almost isn't, or what isn't it
is almost what it isn't, couldn't, or what it is,

Touches covering my body and face
Hungry, my body, and soft, etc. Not even conveying disinterest in all that fucking shit

second second

act

ANOTHER MOPE OF INDEFATIGABLE LACK #2

Living, looking up to the stars
or whatever. How your inaudibility bulldozes
shaking me. Bombed city. May we warmly raise
the imaginary necessary architecture,
again.
           Last night, the wilderness
body I inhabited, the important people with dawn rising,
the recurring people, and I, immediate
luxurious cloud inches away, able to be
nothing but alone, unable to receive
the enormous coherence,
sobbing a musical purge or something, only
sky within the morning, and within
the night also, too.

please Fuck hold me, throwing my body
onto you, when not even I myself know it, change
not ever occurring on its own.
                        & there are people to whom
you are important, you
have to think, to push
shaking through recurring streets
toward some marvelous experience in the muffled
morning.
           & last night, tasting
yourself on hatchet lips, your expression illuminatedly changed.
You were foolishly important all of a sudden, sudden
snow, hysterical cling, inside
your sweater that you didn't take off me so I did, my body hurled onto
you.

The dawn way I have to be held, instead
distilled. Toward deeply the end. 90% off, or whatever.
I am even unable to have breakfast, being simply
the enormous West; McDonald's makes me
insane meat blood:
                              I have to Fuck imitate the uh quiet,
through absolutely transparent water, rock that I am,
disorder my holding or whatever & astonishingly cavernous. I imagine that
ghosts are warm. And O'Hara in his fragile sadness too, his dumped body
glistening on mine, it helps me flee
the hunter.

       & please   P
       -lay with me
       On the quiet
       streets Under
       Eventually
       The stars

YOU LOL'ED AT MY DREAMS

I asked you on facebook chat what were the most important things to you
and you were like, do you mean in life, like, in general? or professionally or what?
and I said, no, just in general, like, what is most important to you
and you didn't answer me you were like "i don't fucking know"

and part of me asking you a question sincerely
is to hear you answer it sincerely
but that's okay
another part of it is to have you ask me back that same question sincerely
and that you didn't ask it is okay too

in my head I was like, happiness, peace, love are the most important things to me
like, for everyone to be happy and loving and peaceful or close to it
like, I can't see any reason why countries shouldn't just peacefully coexist
or like, I don't see any reason why the designation of "country" can't simply be
                              administrative as opposed to competitive
like, shit like that
like, society is fucking making fucking making us into fucking "docile bodies"
who don't question authority or laws that are actually stupid and/or fucked

I wanted to have a conversation about shit like that

later you asked me what my dreams were
and I didn't realize that you were being sarcastic
and when I told you that it was for everyone to be happy you typed "LOL"
and I typed "fuck you"
and I closed the chat and looked for someone else to chat with

Sec Interm

ond

ission

TRILOGY

HEART MOPE

OBITUARY

CHARITY

HEART MOPE

heart

              is (The linkage no longer, try,

      and have tried, and tried.)

the only beginning,

      light on, off—off.
                    (chip in mouth
        So: to find   until found, then unfound.

Or found.   here is he, yawning n the corner, shadowed light
      annotating   rain on street
            lips   n ontological apprehension.

& ze absolutely worthless understood as, myself and all it signifies or nearly,
Bullet Shank Raped Inalienable rights *Machine* à Shit *laver* Wound.
how the only to discover amazing here it is thing, near-perceptible, near.

& here, you, are, of course are, period, trought to find. Fund.
Coughing, n the corner, millimeter beard's growth, kiss. Found.
lips. —on, hip to hip, cock to ass, on, this. Smile when I look. At you. Stunned.

& Let the flowerclouds burst revelingly in of love our and bruisedly water too
                           glisten ground
Let the is amplify delirium Sense And Mechanism Body Sick Datum Priority

     & no—   shooting star, baby born.

only fleetingly scene   bombs falls, on

      and n the light off red   the glow, (food,

the meat heated up, knife cuts hot slice, pagination, the heart normal on, crunch

OBITUARY

exhaustedness, freedom
being the critical most thing,
must leapt the crystal prison walls. I believe
thru fool of plant and romping branch resting leapt I can

fear to hold our (own
in held) delight pulsating
addressing its importance
                     yet, un, —ever need Shit the light
(shonedness, dilute). somehow soaringly thru kindness sleeping spark of
                                saying I'm alright

obituary for the achievable, for our paradise, long to leapt.
puking up the philly cheesesteak Into the toilet Into the night.

usage invisibility is ending.
and y'all say "love that"
yet show them the music & they cry and writhe and thrash,
modeling what?   —ever need:
yr wisdom, yr ass, the hug support & un:

to be held and) not holding, power leaves the body, interdependence
to build, stupidly and immobilabilibly, Fuck fight (and might
to attack, leapt, laughter. In the friends walker fields form adventure. circling
                               the unicorn.

drained of water and seeds polluted
by our shame by their paper their text unmarrowed,
the story by omission is actionable.
          the meal is assigned to hunger and that's that,
                armor slow in bright
                vicious speed.

you, bending me, til I
       broke,

               joke;
Fuck, do not let us go where beauty
is ghost is simply something
                           (tear
my heart away, try, from restriction attachment, and single
fallen tombstone of the persearchering barred "body" into which yr cock,
love, unoftenedly had entered thru close hope repair not knowing who's
responsible
                                 (to endure, dry, drunk with sadness of trying and
shitting rabies of the slowly unfeeling numbingedly Fuck height
(the day never comes
              in absentia or crushingly with technologies like concepts or image
          or food or else like green flesh centered horizontal
              flesh and did I say joy o decimos abundancia
              prosperar bendición

And to be
(perdisgustingly, absolutely) of your economic context with no possibility of
transcending it but all or,
ecclesiastes, some.

CHARITY

Again my
love. Having.

buck for homeless woman,
walk down street.

mountains precedentlessly from molehill forcibly
dynamiteguttedly crammed Fuck *Shit*, with

radioactive waste. nostr'inheritance
"we" "have".

my cuddles wriggling.
sun downstream.

& Herewith
I love you,

forcing my face into my vomit.
I love you too,

which, precisely, is not enough.

You must read our disgusting poetry,

which is not for sale, & disorder
your daily jogging charitable billionaire enthusiasm mutilatedly fuckface

now. i am amassing
faggot-brown limb buckets. i am dumping

them bloodily on the Power steps. Power
-bottom steps.
                          See? For them it's not enough.

Shirtlessly on the grass, even sunlight
on zir back. Marketlessly.

even the gifts we gave each other together—we—
from tenderness?

from anyone?
to meet a need?

what was mobility terror for,
then?

& class hatred under the moonlight?

I'll say a gift is
mutual creation,

not the about-to-be-ness of the
petite bourgeoisie before the moment

of reception. A transaction. Again, which is the wrong
again, cavernously from. I *know* this.

    sooooooooooooooo zooming the tiniest distance is actually
    enormous, we

    shall try, shall we try to eliminate
    distance? so that I am

    right beside
    you or inside

    you, whatever given everything we have given
    to create third from the forcibly space?

SOME MOPES

I always want
What I can have Pet
the water
Next to me Be
with me Grow
stubble freely on the weekends

I shave & I work
Google search <3
Print the map Everywhere
love is commodified
/ life is cheap but tulips must be paid for

You must make
this poem A paper plane
Soaring Thirsty Desirc violent

When it is no longer in sight We will have change

CAPITAL
for you

Your being in the world is your ability.
Your role, mobility occur in the mind, too.

Beside your "brook"
edited by leisure, which for you is just your brook, but whose

contents i must fucking stab
towards out unalienatedly.

Musteth i cannibalize your normalized fuckface?

Either way, then, you are
absurd. Working

at your job. Into the meter, the coin that
you insert. My knife,

which I do have, into our minutely life,
it raises the Other into the "ass"-fucking One.

Hence, the flesh is the medium, that
by which i have known, theretofore, what

it am to "be", arealessness. Denied my own sphere
color or

whatever. *A* white, *E* white, *U*
white, *O* white, so i faggotly vomit the white meat i ate,

writing the roar of blood? Unto documented "you"?

My object blood
bones roaring on quaking the platter, then, articulately. Either way.

The icicles plummets, which i, and you, could never possess.
But you can. And because you do, I will force you

explodingly into the beautiful microwave.

All stabable desire by nurture
to mutilate invisibility. Own

my, systemic my,
what reproduces you and gives me potentiality

only, jizzing my invaluably into
your content, i'm thrilled to say, face,

race,
space,

pzace,
where Virus mind-blowingly

spread.

Since you are seeking this knowledge,
restaurant with your classed tissue, content

you, you have security
that i do not have, capital which

you possess
silently, i fucking screaming.

PHORO

When I first started learning to fly planes I never thought I'd help contact a never-
before-contacted indigenous peoples in the Amazon
John took photos of them
And when we came back to take more photos they were covered in red war paint and
shooting arrows at us

The ... woman was covered in black paint and she wasn't holding anything
She was standing watching us
Incredible

All the red on my body is because of you
John, all the black on my body is because of you

*

i'm not fucking done with you
y'all get to write your bullshit
in my mind and thru my body
and I can't hack and hack for 5 more and hack spreads?

PULITZER MOPE

I will win awards for my ability
to express my debilitating
loneliness beautifully.

Moreover, I hope
wanting you makes me
write critically acclaimed mopes forever & forever mope.

Life may be as easy as that. I want,
& tweet my despair to the buying world,
cum out my loneliness, &c.

LAMBDA MOPE

I see your boyfriend.
And I hate him.
When he calls you and you answer and I tell you to tell him hi and you tell him
hi and you tell me he doesn't say anything back I feel like unloading a
hot steaming litany of corn-ed bowel movements unto his face.

I would actually love to give you head, and like, care for you, if you wanted.
Dump the clown / live in gloriousness with me.
plz

ONLY WHEN CONFRONTED WITH EXPLOSIONS DO I SEE ROOM FOR IMPROVEMENT

I know a few instruments;   re beginning is one of them.
                                        It is my ringtone.

My app says   if you are loving and he is not   enough,
perhaps you should be leaving,   perhaps you have had enough.

I will tell next him that I like him   and he will not need   to reply quickly
It will be enough for me to count the beautiful things I can see   then kiss   :)

I watch a video from the beginning all the way through
                                        to the end and I am
                                                    not b
                                                         o
                                                    r   I   a
                                                    e   m
                                                    d.   l
I watch another video and then I laugh a little bit. When I laugh, I realize   aughing.

Maybe improving with explosions,   before I realize it's a bomb,
before it formalizes,   —nah just observing someone sry I'm listening.

It's like I am hearing my loneliness every time I click   or clack.
It's like ...20 dollars—   d'you want me to buy it for you? Yeah—thanks.

Just fuckin', fuckin', just come, get pizza with me or something.   I'll pay /
                                        Get on your knees, little bitch.
Search, Find, Like: A kind of refreshed life.

The colonial adjectives of my current possessions: eh & meh,   But I care
about   so much, you can see me cry about it when I sleep

&   in the incessant cultivation of possibility that that makes. For ex.
away from the nice & commodified & towards the sweaty bow & an unbowing & each mini-
bow bead unbows the big one, the bow that is, & look there are a million presents I am
offering you   with   me among them

Only when confronted with explosions do you see   room for improvement
Be there in 20   & then I ate pizza with the person eating pizza

pizza pizza pizza   **pizza pizza**
pizza pizza pizza pizza   pizza pizza pizza **pizza**
 pizza pizza pizza pizza pizza   pizza pizza pizza **pizza**
 pizza pizza pizza pizza pizza pizza   pizza pizza pizza pizza **pizza**
   pizza pizza pizza pizza pizza pizza pizza pizza pizza pizza pizza **pizza**
   pizza pizza pizza pizza pizza pizza pizza pizza pizza pizza pizza **pizza**
   pizza pizza pizza pizza pizza pizza pizza pizza pizza pizza pizza **pizza**
   pizza pizza pizza pizza pizza pizza pizza pizza pizza pizza pizza **pizza**
   pizza pizza pizza pizza pizza pizza pizza pizza pizza pizza pizza **pizza**
    pizza pizza pizza pizza pizza pizza pizza pizza pizza pizza **pizza**
     pizza pizza pizza pizza pizza pizza pizza pizza **pizza**
      pizza pizza pizza pizza pizza pizza **pizza**
       pizza pizza pizza pizza pizza **pizza**
        pizza pizza **pizza**
         pizza

aaaaaaaaaaaaaaaaaaaaaaaaaaaaaaaaaaaaaaaaaaaaaaaaaaaaaandI got into my bed and slept—

AND WHAT CLEAR STREAM

shit on my warm tender heart & make me vomit looking for love
                forever besmirch beat down to death in all the right places
and drop curving up to stomach no dick in any angle acute
                     and the skin around it with heat's lack insensitive
sparkling faces growth gluttony shitted babies &
                massive population extermination the hard flush's favor
and wet cheek drop falling yellowy tear apart to touch nothing
            flower urine tongue nothing crude acne ugh nothing 2 run from cum
run from cum never touch one another only take
issue hazel eyes smoke in vomit in each vast meadow riot in the pesticide worm heart
                  weathervane tinkles on glorious porch sunlit punch
memorize German vocabulary & *Fahrt* & shit

difficult the dream to kiss from difficult this distance from afar no word 'kiss' Fuck.
        flowing stream wiping cream weeping to make the daily moping art clean
to love and dance and fuck *à la mode*
             bike tracks in the snow
                it seems that he creates a building
      declining & lip plump
2 eliminate dissident elements around my road
             kill & smell my rotting architecture delicious melt
and if i am to survive my pulsating heart mortar from afar burst body
        to form new wholes *en masse* which is exactly to bomb the wheel
to push down the existing landscape to make room for the job that is being down
            up blow i find what this druggingly recreational not high but
cynical estimates 2 never preserve low civilization
        r yum the or the but yes the or the no but and so no but the
bird that's flown into the room
           yellow-breasted shut dictionary slut up cut
and electrocuted til charred and unsinging

                  & y r u so beautiful?
kissable your profile pictures tiny heart i gaping need your Fuck. Shove
                        to mind read & *Schwulsein ist nur eine andere*
Art zu lieben unvisible pantingly hungry don't you kept-inside notice aside step Fuck.
                        und Liebe ist die schönste Art, fuck *glücklich zu sein*
& is the heart a grave
                invisible digital blow job at the atomic level
intense proliferation of quotidian desire
                            eyes my closed and to onto your face cum and shit
              I love you

& why resist at all
            'open-shirtedly happy-trailedly possible' is as equally valid as 'fair game'
and the time between now and now is
                        as unalterably simple as 'the time after now'
when why protest at all
                is simply alterable:
"Okay. Use the thing," she said.
                     & b 4 i can continue shitting in the most great sadness
& everyone barebacks and gets and AIDS
              & and they all die and
and you are alive allowed for and by the culture and the & the institutions
                  and that and and cater to and you
& sometimes the air is so marvelous overwhelmingly
              shit that you shoot your accustomed dove
—Shove.

M O P E S ← P O E M S

With TREMENDOUS gratitude for

Rebecca Wolff, Jean-Jacques Poucel, Matias
Viegener, and God.

Without the Wassaic Project, the Studios
at MASS MoCA, the California Institute of
the Arts, Crosstown Arts, and Jonah Wolf
/ the Wolf Residency, assembling this
manuscript might not have been possible.

Kevin Holden, David Gorin, Josh Stanley,
Edgar Garcia, so much love to you all.

To Sam Haft for the seeds of DISSPOEM,
to Greg Nissan for the positive
reinforcement, to Nina Menkes, Roberto
Tejada, and Michael Leong for your
inspiration by example, thank you.
Shoutout Ramon Tejada, dream collaborator
& paradigm.

But for real—Rebecca.

Thanks, y'all.

The "selfless devotion to duty" quotation
is from Andrei Tarkovsky's *Sculpting
in Time*, as translated by Kitty Hunter-
Blair, from the essay "The artist's
responsibility."

Thanks for reading *MOPES*.